Your Final Destination

Printed in the United States of America

ISBN: 9798354398300

Create Space

Contents

Other Books by the Author

Moments of Truth
8-Lane Highway
God's Plan for Your Finances
Thirsty for Water
Angels of God
On Fire Illustrations and Stories
The Believers Boot Camp
Old, Wrinkled and Closer to Heaven
The Hand of God
Living in the Hand of God
Trusting in the Hand of God
Grieving like a King
Amazing Young People
A Million Grains of Sand
The Eleven11 Project
What About Dinosaurs?
Why Jesus Wept
L.O.S.T. People Matter
OMEGA DAYS – A World on Edge
Walking in a New Way of Life
OMEGA DAYS – The Beginning of the End
Strange Phenomenon's
ONE WORLD #1 – Wave of Terror
ONE WORLD #2 – Wave of Destruction
ONE WORLD #3 – Eagle Down

This book asks the question...

"Where will you spend eternity"

"Your Final Destination"

Rev. Danny Formhals

<u>Dedication</u>

To the wonderful people at Highway Worship Center in Fruitland, Idaho. May we experience the harvest, a mighty revival, and long years of great fellowship together.

Revelation 1:3 (NKJV)
"Blessed is he who reads and those who hear the words of this prophecy, and keep those things which are written in it; for the time is near."

"Stay faithful until the end."

A Message from Pastor Danny

The contents of this book are no joking matter. The place you will spend eternity should be the most critical thought in your heart and mind. Jesus said, *"What will it profit a man if he gains the whole world, and loses his own soul? Or what will a man give in exchange for his soul?"* (Mark 8:36-37).

You matter to God

Because you matter to God and us, the information inside these pages will literally help determine Your Final Destination.

I want you to know how valuable you are to the Lord. Make no mistake; Jesus suffered on the cross for you (Matt. 27:31-35). He gave His life as a ransom, paying your debt (2 Tim. 2:3-6). He traded His life for yours. That is why you matter to the Lord and why your eternal soul is worth everything to Him. He paid the ultimate price so you wouldn't have to (John 3:16).

You have two choices

Like everyone, you only have two choices. The first is Heaven, and the second is its opposite, hell. While hell was initially prepared for the Devil and his angels (Matt. 25:41). Heaven is meant for you. Jesus

I promise, it will be worth it

went to prepare a place for you (John 14:1-4); if you are willing to accept Him and, equally important, live for Him. So let me be clear, biblically, you cannot acknowledge Jesus with your lips in the church and then go out into the world and deny him by an opposite lifestyle.

Heaven is an actual place, and those with a personal relationship with Jesus Christ will enjoy it all eternity long.

Sadly, those who reject the free gift of eternal life, which comes ONLY through Jesus Christ (Acts 4:12) will walk themselves into hell (Rev. 21:8). These people are called unbelievers.

My sincere plea

I have dedicated my life to serving the Lord. I love Him because He first loved me (1 John 4:19). Because I love the Lord, I love you. I plead with you to open your mind (Acts 26:18; Col. 3:2) to Jesus. I implore you to open your heart (Rev. 3:20) to Jesus. Will you give Him a real opportunity to revolutionize your life?

He is waiting to bless, heal, change, give you hope, and so much more. Will you embrace the Savior and give Him a chance, a real opportunity to touch and change your life? I promise it will be worth it. So, don't breathe your last breath on earth without considering the pages of this book.

—

Hebrews 9:27-28

"It is appointed for men to die once, but after this the judgment, so Christ was offered once to bear the sins of many. To those who eagerly wait for Him He will appear a second time, apart from sin, for salvation."

It is my great pleasure to aid you in making a NEW commitment to Jesus Christ. The plan of salvation, beginning on page 78, ends with a prayer. After you've prayed that prayer, according to the Bible, your relationship with Jesus has just begun. Of course, we (the church where you received this book) are here to answer any of your questions and to pray with you. I hope to guide you into living a committed relationship with Jesus Christ once you are saved.

Here's the good news and what God says to you. It's found in 2 Cor. 6:2, *"At the right time I heard your prayers. On the day of salvation, I helped you. I tell you that the right time is now, and the day of salvation is now."*

Pastor Danny Formhals

Your Final Destination

Rev. Danny L. Formhals

Stuff About

HEAVEN

"But God made a promise to us, and we are waiting for a new heaven and a new earth where goodness lives"
- 2 Peter 3:13 (NCV)

Your Final Destination

1

Quotes about Heaven

1. **Missing Heaven** – "<u>YOU</u> do not want to miss heaven. <u>GOD</u> does not want you to miss heaven. <u>I</u> do not want you to miss heaven. You do not <u>HAVE</u> to miss heaven" – *Bob Farley*

2. **Jesus is enough** – "For the Christian, heaven is where Jesus is. We do not need to speculate on what heaven will be like. It is

enough to know that we will be forever with Him" – *William Barclay*

3. **Heaven is better than earth** – "To go to heaven, fully to enjoy God, is infinitely better than the most pleasant accommodations here" – *Jonathan Edwards*

4. **One moment in Heaven** – "I would not give one moment of heaven for all the joy and riches of the world, even if it lasted for thousands and thousands of years" – *Martin Luther*

5. **Joy** – "Joy is the serious business of Heaven" – *C.S. Lewis*

6. **Heaven worthwhile** – "God never said that the journey would be easy, but He did say that the arrival would be worthwhile" – *Max Lucado*

7. **Just Traveling** – "My home is in Heaven. I'm just traveling through this world" – *Billy Graham*

8. **Unsurpassed Joy** – "Scripture repeatedly makes clear that heaven is a realm of unsurpassed joy, unfading glory, undiminished bliss, unlimited delights, and unending pleasures. Nothing about it can possibly be boring or humdrum. It will be a

perfect existence. We will have unbroken fellowship with all heaven's inhabitants. Life there will be devoid of any sorrows, cares, tear, fears, or pain" – *John MacArthur*

9. **Good morning** – "We'll say good night here and good morning up there" – *John R. Rice*

10. **Stay ready** – "Jesus when to prepare Heaven for you. The lest you can do it stay prepared and ready for Him" – *Danny L. Formhals*

11. **Perfect happiness** – "God will prepare everything for our perfect happiness in heaven, and if it takes my dog being there, I believe he'll be there" – *Billy Graham*

12. **No heaven by works** – "One of the most staggering truths of the Scriptures is to understand that we do not earn our way to heaven. ...works have a place--but as a demonstration of having received God's forgiveness, not as a badge of merit of having earned it" – *Ravi Zacharias*

Your Final Destination

13. **Heaven is a holy place** – "Without holiness on earth we shall never be prepared to enjoy heaven. Heaven is a holy place. The Lord of heaven is a holy Being. The angels are holy creatures. Holiness is written on everything in heaven... How shall we ever be at home and happy in heaven if we die unholy?" – *J.C. Ryle*

14. **I'm more alive than ever** – "Someday you will read in the papers that D.L. Moody of East Northfield, is dead. Don't you believe a word of it! At that moment I shall be more alive than I am now; I shall have gone up higher, that is all, out of this old clay tenement into a house that is immortal- a body that death cannot touch, that sin cannot taint; a body fashioned like unto His glorious body" – *Dwight L. Moody*

15. **Heaven in the soul** – "Heaven will be inherited by every man who has heaven in his soul." – *Henry Ward Beecher*

16. **Looking forward** – "A continual looking forward to the eternal world is not a form of escapism or wishful thinking, but one of the things a Christian is meant to do." – *C.S. Lewis*

15

17. **Store up treasures in Heaven** – "Many Christians dread the thought of leaving this world. Why? Because so many have stored up their treasures on earth, not in heaven. Each day brings us closer to death. If your treasures are on earth, that means each day brings you closer to losing your treasures" – *Randy Alcorn*

18. **How sweet** – "How sweet is rest after fatigue! How sweet will heaven be when our journey is ended" – *George Whitefield*

19. **Jesus is enough** – "Depend upon it, your dying hour will be the best hour you have ever known! Your last moment will be your richest moment, better than the day of your birth will be the day of your death. It shall be the beginning of heaven, the rising of a sun that shall go no more down forever!" – *C.H. Spurgeon*

20. **I must go** – "Earth recedes. Heaven opens before me. If this is death, it is sweet! There is no valley here. God is calling me, and I must go" – *D.L. Moody*

2

Stories about Heaven

All over the world people have gone to heaven and were sent back to tell the world about it. Their real-life testimony provides solid and undeniable proof of heaven.

90 Minutes in Heaven – Don Piper, who was pronounced clinically dead after a car crash in 1989, said he traveled to heaven. After paramedics pulled his lifeless body from a four-car pile-up, Piper found himself "standing at some magnificent gates surrounded by people I had known and loved in life. So, when I saw them, I knew where I was, because I knew where they were. There really are a lot of magnificent structures inside the gate. And at the pinnacle of a great hill beyond them is a bright light."

Grandmother in Heaven – After being T-boned by a teen driver who ran a red light, Julie Papievis found herself in a coma due to a serious brain stem injury, and she wasn't expected to survive. While doctors and her family debated about how to proceed, Papievis became acquainted with the afterlife. She told the *700 Club*: "It was so vast, and there was no real beginning or end to it. It was just perfect peace. It was like I was home, and I wanted to stay there." But apparently it wasn't her time. As Papievis recalled, "My grandmother said, 'No, you can't come with us. You have to go back. Go back and be happy.'" Ten years later, she recovered enough to complete a triathlon.

Heaven is for Real – Heaven is for Real is probably the most famous account of an otherworldly visit, and it comes to us from Colton Burpo, who was only 3 years old when he perished on the operating table during an emergency appendectomy. He allegedly went to heaven, then returned with knowledge of a great-

grandfather he never met and an unborn, miscarried sister. He also saw Jesus riding a rainbow-colored horse.

The Throne of God — In the early 20th century, a woman named Mrs. Jang who lived in the Shan Tung province of North China reportedly succumbed to tuberculosis after becoming a born-again Christian, but she didn't stay dead. Instead, she says she went to heaven: "I saw many beautiful houses all of pretty colors. I walked beside the Lord on the golden streets... Then we went on and I saw thousands of angels in a circle, singing and playing lovely music. In the midst was the throne of glory. The Heavenly Father sat upon it, and when I saw Him, I was afraid. I hardly dared to lift my eyes."

Sat on Jesus Lap — As if chronic intestinal pseudo-obstruction doesn't sound bad enough, Annabel Beam suffered a serious accident at the age of 9 when she fell head-first into a hollow cottonwood tree and was stuck for several hours, including some time unconscious. Eventually firefighters pulled her to safety.

A day after the incident, Annabel told her mother Christy that she "sat on Jesus's lap" and shared how Jesus told her there were still goals for her to complete on earth, and that she'd be healed. Initially, Christy didn't believe her, but when Annabel dropped some knowledge about her mom's two miscarriages, she knew her daughter had somehow visited the afterlife and wasn't simply suffering from a delusion. Annabel immediately recovered from her longtime intestinal disorder, which doctors couldn't explain. She has since had a movie made about her life starring Jennifer Garner, called Miracles from Heaven.

I Watched My Life like a Movie – Sondra Abrahams, a self-described "pew warmer," passed at the age of 30 from an allergic reaction to medication after an operation. As she went into cardiac arrest in the emergency room, Abrahams claimed she could see herself dying as she started rising up through the ceiling. Then she felt pulled "from one dimension to another" where she ran straight into Jesus, who put his arms around her soul and then played her life back for her like a movie: "I saw every time I did something good and I felt His love and joy. When I did something bad, I felt His hurt and intense pain that I caused Him. He showed me my whole life. But He never stopped loving me." After a short chat with Jesus, they decided she would go back to earth and fight to help overturn Roe v. Wade.

The place was pain free – Anita Moorjani, a public speaker, was diagnosed with lymphoma in 2002 and was quickly losing her battle to cancer. She had withered down to 85 pounds and battling tumors from the base of her skull to her abdomen. In February 2006, she slipped into a coma. It was then that Anita says she underwent a near-death experience. Anita said, *"I felt as though I was above my body,"* she said. *"It was like I had 360-degree peripheral vision of the whole area around. But not just in the room where my body was in, but beyond the room."*

During the experience, Anita was reunited with her father, who shared with her that she had gone as far as she can go. If she decided to go any further, she wouldn't be able to turn back. Anita, however, didn't want to turn back and return to Earth, because the place that she had visited was incredibly beautiful and pain-free.

Anita said that *"all of the discomfort and fear of life was gone,"* and she simply felt incredible, with feelings of *"unconditional love."* Anita said she felt this sense of overwhelming, incredible clarity *"where everything started to make sense."*

So, she decided to return to Earth and her body because she had this inner knowing that her body would heal very quickly. And it did. Within four days of waking up from her coma, her tumors shrunk by 70 percent, and physicians were in disbelief. It was a miracle.

There was nothing negative allowed – Many people heard about Mickey Robinson's experience after nearly being killed in a plane crash in 1968 before his parachute jump. The plane's engine stopped and hit an oak tree face first. Robinson then found himself surrounded by darkness and he felt the terror of eternal hell. He asked God to give him a second chance and immediately he was rushed into the Lord's presence. "There was nothing negative allowed to be in the presence of God. So, I was pure and I was innocent. And it's so incredible the ecstasy, the bliss, the joy, all the stuff we've read about, when you really experience it, we don't have words," he described. Robinson was given a mission from God to tell people there is hope and they can be forgiven.

The Kingdom of God is closer than we think – Steven R. Musick was a young man in the Navy when he suffered an allergic reaction to a vaccine for the swine flu. His heart stopped and he entered the presence of Jesus. Heaven was vibrant with colors and words could not describe the love He felt when he found himself face-to-face with the risen Christ! Musick shared that Christ looked young and radiated with a light. Jesus walked Musick through fields of flowing grass and reviewed his life since he was born. Musick discovered that Christ was always the bridge to the Creator after the encounter. Now, a financial planner, Musick travels the country to share the love of Christ that he experienced and also wrote the book *Life After Heaven*. "I began to see my life from the perspective of Heaven," he said. "The Kingdom of Heaven is closer than we think."

Transferred to the Church Triumphant

A place of stillness – Diver Ian McCormack was stung by jellyfish and died and went to Heaven and hell. Meanwhile, his mother saw an image of her son in front of her and was led by God to pray. During this time, McCormack flatlined and was clinically dead for over 15 minutes. McCormack called out to God and a light submerged into the darkness where he encountered an astonishing sense of peace. The more McCormack acknowledged his sins before God, the more love he felt. The diver also shared that Heaven was attractive, luminous and a place of stillness. When he woke up in the morgue, a doctor was taking a blade to his body. McCormack's eyes shot open and God whispered that He gave his life back! Guess what happened next? He walked out the hospital the next day.

Heaven is beautiful – Brian Miller was an Ohio truck driver and he felt a tightness in his chest driving to a delivery one night. What happened next was hair-raising. His heart suddenly stopped beating for 45 minutes and first responders feared that he would suffer irreversible brain damage and possibly become brain dead. While he was struggling to remain on earth, Miller said he saw a light and described how beautiful Heaven was. He then ran into his mother-in-law, who had just passed away just days before. "She was the most beautiful thing when I saw her, just like the day I first met her," he recounted. She also had a message for him: "It's not your time. You don't need to be here," she told him. "We need to take you back. You have things to do at home."

(Stories taken from Ranker.com and beliefnet.com)

3

What the Bible says about Heaven

All Scriptures taken from the NJKV

⬆ **Our citizenship is in heaven** – *"For our citizenship is in heaven, from which we also eagerly wait for the Savior, the Lord Jesus Christ, 21 who will trans- form our lowly body that it may be conformed to His glorious body, according to the working by which He is able even to subdue all things to Himself"* (Phil. 14:1-3).

⬆ **Jesus is preparing heaven for His followers** – *"In My Father's house are many mansions;*

if it were not so, I would have told you. I go to prepare a place for you" (John 14:2-3).

⬆ **Few people will enter heaven** – *"Enter by the narrow gate; for wide is the gate and broad is the way that leads to destruction, and there are many who go in by it. 14 Because narrow is the gate and difficult is the way which leads to life, and there are few who find it"* (Matt. 7:13-14).

⬆ **Death will not exist in heaven** – *"He will swallow up death forever, And the Lord God will wipe away tears from all faces; The rebuke of His people He will take away from all the earth; For the Lord has spoken"* (Isa. 25:8).

⬆ **Our lives will not be complete until we enter heaven** – *"For we know that if our earthly house, this tent, is destroyed, we have a building from God, a house not made with hands, eternal in the heavens. 2 For in this we groan, earnestly desiring to be clothed with our habitation which is from heaven"* (2 Cor. 5:2).

⬆ **Heaven is much better than earth** – *"For I am hard pressed between the two, having a desire to depart and be with Christ, which is far better"* (Phil.1:23).

⬆ **There will not be any sadness in heaven** – *"God will wipe away every tear from their eyes; there shall be no more death, nor sorrow, nor crying. There shall be no more pain, for the former things have passed away"* (Rev. 21:4).

⬆ **Jesus is in Heaven with God** – *"This is a faithful saying: For if we died with Him, we shall also live with Him. If we endure, we shall also reign with Him"* (2 Tim. 2:11-12).

⬆ **Believers receive a crown in heaven** –

"Do I have fought the good fight, I have finished the race, I have kept the faith. 8 Finally, there is laid up for me the crown of righteousness, which the Lord, the righteous Judge, will give to me on that Day, and not to me only but also to all who have loved His appearing" (2 Tim. 4:7-8).

⬆ **Christians should look forward to heaven** - *"If then you were raised with Christ, seek those things which are above, where Christ is, sitting at the right hand of God. Set your mind on things above, not on things on the earth. For you died, and your life is hidden with Christ in God. When Christ who is our life appears, then you also will appear with Him in glory"* (Col. 3:1- 5).

⬆ **Heaven is the home of righteousness** - *"Nevertheless we, according to His promise, look for new heavens and a new earth in which righteousness dwells"* (2 Pet.3:13).

⬆ **God is the focus of attention in heaven** - *"For the Lamb who is in the midst of the throne will shepherd them and lead them to living fountains of waters. And God will wipe away every tear from their eyes"* (Rev. 7:17).

⬆ **People in heaven will walk with God** – *"For There shall be no night there: They need no lamp nor light of the sun, for the Lord God gives them light. And they shall reign forever and ever"* (Rev. 22:5).

⬆ **In God's presence there is joy** – *"For You will show me the path of life; In Your presence is fullness of* *joy; At Your right hand are pleasures forevermore"* (Ps. 16:11).

⬆ **God is in heaven** – *"For thus says the Lord: "Heaven is My throne, and earth is My footstool"* (Isa. 66:1).

⬆ **God watches us from heaven** – *"The Lord is in His holy temple, The Lord's throne is in heaven; His eyes behold, His eyelids test the sons of men"* (Ps. 11:4).

⬆ **Heaven is God's dwelling place** – *"For Look down from Your holy habitation, from heaven, and bless Your people Israel and the land which You have given us, just as You swore to our fathers, "a land flowing with milk and honey"* (Deut. 26:15).

⬆ **Heaven is a reward** – *"Rejoice and be exceedingly glad, for great is your reward in heaven"* (Matt. 5:12).

⬆ **Store up treasures for yourself in heaven** – *"Do not lay up for yourselves treasures on earth, where moth and rust destroy and where thieves break in and steal; but lay up for yourselves treasures in heaven, where neither moth nor rust destroys and where thieves do not break in and steal. For where your treasure is, there your heart will be also"* (Matt. 6:19-20).

⬆ **There are angels in heaven** – *"Take heed that you do not despise one of these little ones, for I say to you that in heaven their angels always see the face of My Father who is in heaven"* (Matt. 18:10).

⬆ **Jesus is in Heaven with God** – *"So then, after the Lord had spoken to them, He was received up into heaven, and sat down at the right hand of God"* (Mark 16:19).

⬆ **Heaven rejoices when a sinner repents** – *"I say to you that likewise there will be more* *joy in heaven over one sinner who repents than over ninety-nine just persons who need no repentance"* (Luke 15:7).

⬆ **Heaven is fill with people from all tribes and nations** – *"You After these things I looked, and behold, a great multitude which no one could number, of all nations, tribes, peoples, and tongues, standing before the throne and before the Lamb, clothed with white robes, with palm branches in their hands, 10 and crying out with a loud voice, saying, "Salvation belongs to our God who sits on the throne, and to the Lamb!"* (Rev.7:9).

⬆ **God created all things including heaven** – *"For by Him all things were created that are in heaven and that are on earth, visible and invisible, whether thrones or dominions or principalities or powers. All things were created through Him and for Him"* (Col. 1:16).

⬆ **Jesus will return one day from heaven** – *"Wait for His Son from heaven, whom He raised from the dead, even Jesus who delivers us from the wrath to come"* (1 Thess. 1:10).

⬆ **In heaven we will eat from the Tree of Life** – *"He who has an ear, let him hear what the Spirit says to the churches. To him who overcomes I will give to eat from the tree of life, which is in the midst of the Paradise of God"* (Rev. 2:7).

⬆ **Believers go directly to heaven** – *"Jesus said to him, "Assuredly, I say to you, today you will be with Me in Paradise"* (Luke 23:43).

30

⬆ You will receive a new body in heaven
– "*So when this corruptible has put on incorruption, and this mortal has put on immortality, then shall be brought to pass the saying that is written: "Death is swallowed up in victory." "O Death, where is your sting? O Hades, where is your victory?" The sting of death is sin, and the strength of sin is the law. But thanks be to God, who gives us the victory through our Lord Jesus Christ*" (1 Cor. 15:54-57).

⬆ God is with us here and forever in heaven
– "*If Yea, though I walk through the valley of the shadow of death, I will fear no evil; For You are with me; Your rod and Your staff, they comfort me. You prepare a table before me in the presence of my enemies; You anoint my head with oil; My cup runs over. Surely goodness and mercy shall follow me All the days of my life; And I will dwell in the house of the Lord Forever*" (Ps. 23:4-6).

⬆ Eternal life is forever
– "*Jesus said to her, "I am the resurrection and the life. He who believes in Me, though he may die, he shall live. And whoever lives and believes in Me shall never die. Do you believe this?*" (John 11:25-26).

⬆ God is the focus of attention in heaven
– "*Blessed be the God and Father of our Lord Jesus Christ, who according to His abundant mercy has begotten us again to a living hope through the resurrection of Jesus Christ from the dead, to an inheritance incorruptible and undefiled and that does not fade away, reserved in heaven for you, who are kept by the power of God through faith for salvation ready to be revealed in the last time*" (1 Pet. 1:3-5).

⬆ There are thrones in heaven
– "*And I saw thrones, and they sat on them, and judgment was committed to them. Then I saw the souls of those who had been beheaded for*

31

their witness to Jesus and for the word of God, who had not worshiped the beast or his image, and had not received his mark on their foreheads or on their hands. (Revelation 20:4a). Christians can be confident of life after death - Blessed We are confident, yes, well pleased rather to be absent from the body and to be present with the Lord" (2 Cor. 5:8).

⬆ Everything is made new in heaven –

"Now I saw a new heaven and a new earth, for the first heaven and the first earth had passed away. Also, there was no more sea. Then I, John, saw the holy city, New Jerusalem, coming down out of heaven from God, prepared as a bride adorned for her husband. And I heard a loud voice from heaven saying, "Behold, the tabernacle of God is with men, and He will dwell with them, and they shall be His people. God Himself will be with them and be their God. And God will wipe away every tear from their eyes; there shall be no more death, nor sorrow, nor crying. There shall be no more pain, for the former things have passed away" (Rev. 21:1-5).

⬆ Your name must be found in the Book

– "At that time Michael shall stand up, the great prince who stands watch over the sons of your people; And there shall be a time of trouble, such as never was since there was a nation, even to that time. And at that time your people shall be delivered, everyone who is found writ- ten in the book. And many of those who sleep in the dust of the earth shall awake, Some to everlasting life, Some to shame and everlasting contempt. Those who are wise shall shine Like the brightness of the firmament, and those who turn many to righteousness Like the stars forever and ever. "But you, Daniel, shut up the words, and seal

the book until the time of the end; many shall run to and fro, and knowledge shall increase" (Dan. 12:1-4).

 **Thousand-year reign with Christ** – *"And they lived and reigned with Christ for a thousand years. 5 But the rest of the dead did not live again until the thousand years were finished. This is the first resurrection. 6 Blessed and holy is he who has part in the first resurrection. Over such the second death has no power, but they shall be priests of God and of Christ, and shall reign with Him a thousand years"* (Rev. 21:4b-6).

 **God will separate the sheep from the goats** – *"When the Son of Man comes in His glory, and all the holy angels with Him, then He will sit on the throne of His glory. All the nations will be gathered before Him, and He will separate them one from another, as a shepherd divides his sheep from the goats. And He will set the sheep on His right hand, but the goats on the left"* (Matt. 25:31-33).

 **A New Heaven and a New Earth** – (Rev. 21:1-27).

Rev. Danny L. Formhals

Stuff About
HELL

"Keep yourselves in the love of God, looking for the mercy of our Lord Jesus Christ unto eternal life. And on some have compassion, making a distinction; but others save with fear, pulling them out of the fire"
- Jude 1:21-23

Rev. Danny L. Formhals

4

Quotes about Hell

1. **If there were no Hell** - "If there were no hell, the loss of heaven would be hell." – *Charles Spurgeon*

2. **A pass** - "Those who go to Heaven ride on a pass and enter into blessings that they never earned, but all who go to hell pay their own way." – *John R. Rice*

3. **Company** - "I would rather go to heaven alone than go to hell in company." – *R.A. Torrey*

4. **Jesus taught on Hell** - "The Bible refers to hell a total of 167 times. In Jesus 42 months of public ministry there are 33 recorded instances of Jesus speaking about hell. There is no doubt he warned of hell probably thousands of times." – *Anonymous*

5. **You're going to die** - "I believe that a great number of people are going to die and go to hell because they're counting on their religiosity in the church instead of their relationship with Jesus to get them to heaven. They give lip service to repentance and faith, but they've never been born again." – *Adrian Rogers*

6. **Down to Hell** - "Let us save men by all means under heaven; let us prevent men going down to hell. We are not half as Ernest as we are to be." – *Charles Spurgeon*

7. **Too Late** - "Hell is truth seen too late." – *Thomas Hobbes*

8. **Choices** - "Of all the choice in the world. DON'T GO TO HELL!" – *Danny Formhals*

9. **Hell's high reward** - "Hell is the highest reward that the devil can offer you for being a servant of his." – *Billy Sunday*

10. **A Hell of torment** - "Multitudes of people who expect to go to Heaven will go to a Hell of torment. Thousands of "good" people, "moral" people, church members, even church workers - yes, and, alas, even prophets, priests and preachers - will find themselves lost when they expected to be saved, condemned when they expected approval, cast out of Heaven when they expected to be received into eternal bliss.

That is the explicit meaning of the words of our Lord spoken in Matthew 7:21-23." – *John R. Rice*

11. **God doesn't send you to Hell** - "Don't say that a loving God is going to send you to hell - He's not. The thing that's going to send you to hell is that you're a sinner and you don't want to admit it." – *J. Vernon McGee*

12. **Hell is a long time** - The torments of hell abide forever... If all the earth and sea were sand, and every thousandth year a bird should come, and take away one grain of this sand, it would be a long time ere that vast heap of sand were emptied; yet, if after all that time the damned may come out of hell, there were some hopes; but this word EVER breaks the heart – *Thomas Watson*

13. **Escaping Hell** – "The path to hell is paved with many life choices. The only hope to escape is while you're alive. Once you die, hell will be a place of unending suffering and torment from which there will be no escape." – *Danny L. Formhals*

14. **Imagination** – "It is easier for the imagination to compose a hell with pain than a paradise with pleasure." – *Antoine Rivarol*

 15. **No love there** – "Hell is a place, a time, a consciousness, in which there is no love." – *Richard Bach*

16. **There is a Hell** – "God's grace faces hell's reality straight on, offering full deliverance. Denying hell takes the wind out of grace's sails. If there's no eternal hell, the stakes of redemption are vastly lowered. What exactly did Jesus die to rescue us from?" – *Randy Alcorn*

17. **The wrath of God** – "Wicked men will hereafter earnestly wish to be turned to nothing and forever cease to be that they may escape the wrath of God." – *Jonathan Edwards*

18. **Suffering** – "Suffering in this life is at least partly a warning to us, a foretaste of the eternal suffering we deserve outside of Christ." – *Michael Lawrence*

19. **Remorse** – "God considers it right and suitable that those who rejected Christ see Him triumphant, pure, and justified over all who considered Him unworthy of their trust [Rev. 14:10]. The focus…is not that those in hell have the privilege of seeing what they enjoy, but that they have the remorse of seeing what they rejected." – *John Piper*

20. **A million ages** – "As people listened to Jonathan Edwards preach in the eighteenth century, they were "urged to consider the torment of burning like a livid coal, not for an instant or a day, but for "millions and millions of ages," at the end of which they would know that their torment was no nearer to an end than ever before, and that they would "never, ever be delivered." – *David Platt*

21. **The denial of Hell** – "[The] denial of hell in the name of grace discourages people from the grace [such a person claims to] love, while leading [the individual] toward the hell [one] hates and denies… He who thinks he's not drowning won't reach for the life preserver." – *Randy Alcorn*

22. **Scriptures on hell** – "When you consider that there are 1,850 passages in the New Testament that record Jesus' statements, 13 percent of them are concerned with the theme of everlasting judgment and damnation." – *Mark Driscoll*

23. **The Truth of Damnation** – "Jesus preached more about hell than He did about heaven because He wanted to warn men about the truth of damnation,' says the author." – *John MacArthur*

"On some have compassion, making a distinction; but others save with fear, pulling them out of the fire, hating even the garment defiled by the flesh" (Jude 1:23).

5

Stories about Hell

Strong Sulfur Smell – In May 1997, Jennifer Perez nearly lost her life after a group of friends drugged her soda and attempted to sexually assault her. Perez was hospitalized for three days, where she slipped in and out of consciousness. During this time, Perez claims she floated out of her body. She was led first to heaven, then to hell: "When we stopped, I opened my eyes, and I was standing on a great road. I didn't know where it leads to. But the first thing that I felt there was thirst. I was really thirsty! I kept telling the angel, 'I'm thirsty, I'm thirsty!' But it was like he didn't even hear me. I started to cry, and when the tears ran down my cheeks, they completely evaporated. There was the smell of sulfur, like burning tires. I tried to cover my nose, but that made it even worse. All my five senses were very sensitive. When I tried to cover myself, I could smell the sulfur even more. Also, all those little hairs on my arms, they just disappeared. I felt all the heat, it was very hot." Perez witnessed people being tormented by terrifying demons, and though she tried, she could do nothing to save them. After she was given this glimpse of hell, she was led back to heaven, where God gave her a second chance at life.

Endless Darkness – Angie Fenimore attempted suicide in January 1991 and claims to have visited hell before she was saved. After being subject to a "life review," where she had to relive her entire life as a series of images, she entered hell. At first, all she saw was endless darkness and a group of other young people whom she refers to as "the suicides." She also spent time in a different part of hell where lost

souls rambled through a field, too miserable to interact with one another.

Suspended Over a Fiery Pit – Matthew Botsford was shot in the back of the head outside a restaurant in March 1992. To save his life, doctors put him in a medically induced coma which lasted 27 days. Botsford claimed to have spent that time shackled and dangling over a pit of magma being tormented by terrifying, four-legged creatures who would devour his flesh only to have it grow back to be devoured again. However, he says that worse than all these torments was the profound loneliness and isolation he felt, as every sufferer in hell is totally alone. Eventually, a gigantic hand pulled him out, while a voice said, "It's not your time."

A Battle of Souls – In December 1943, Dr. George Ritchie, who was suffering from pneumonia, perished for nine minutes. Ritchie claims his spirit rose from his hospital bed and glimpsed his dead body below before Jesus escorted him through a tour of the afterlife. One section of hell was reserved for people who can never fulfill their longings. He saw dead people in a bar desperately grasping for drinks, and smokers reaching out for cigarettes in vain. In another part of hell, Ritchie saw a huge fight between souls of the dead, with endless physical conflict and terrible, perverse acts.

A Many-Headed Dragon – In September 1985, 15-year-old Tamara Laroux attempted suicide by shooting herself in the chest. After pulling the trigger, she found herself in a fiery pit, where hundreds of souls were screaming in agony, unable to talk to one another, even though they were crowded together. Laroux also says she saw a creature with dragon-like heads, "fiercer than anything that the earth has ever seen." Then, a shining hand descended and carried her up to heaven, before depositing her back in her own home again. Laroux survived because the bullet missed her heart by a quarter of an inch, and now dedicates her life to teaching others about the truth of hell.

Many Priests Seen in Hell – In April 1985, Father Jose Maniyangat was hit by a drunk driver and nearly lost his life. Maniyangat claims he saw heaven, hell, and purgatory during his near-death experience. He says hell is about 2,000 degrees Fahrenheit and filled with souls screaming in agony. He also says there are seven levels of hell, and you are assigned to a level

47

based on the severity of the sins you have committed. Interestingly, Maniyangat claims to have seen fellow priests and bishops suffering in hell. "Many of them were there because they had misled the people with false teaching and bad example," he says.

23 Minutes in Hell – Bill Wiese claims to have visited hell even though he did not have a near-death experience. Wiese was already a devout Christian who lived a normal, peaceful life. Then, on November 28, 1998, at exactly 3 AM, Wiese was suddenly "plunged into hell." He describes being trapped in a 15-foot-by-10-foot cell with giant, foul-smelling reptile-human creatures who went after him. At last, he woke up in his own bed again at 3:23 AM and dedicated his life to spreading the word that hell is real.

Caves Filled with Torments – A Polish nun named Sister Faustina claimed to have visited hell in 1936. She wrote about the experience in her diary, where she described hell as one torment after another, from eternal darkness to a "terrible suffocating smell." However, the worst torments are psychological - the "perpetual remorse of conscience" and the loss of hope.

In addition to this general despair, there are caves and grottoes equipped with special torments designed for different kinds of sinners. "I would have died at the very sight of these tortures," she writes, "if the omnipotence of God had not supported me."

(Most taken from Ranker.com)

6

What the Bible says about Hell

All Scriptures taken from the NJKV

❧ **The fire in hell is not quenched** – "*And they shall go forth and look Upon the corpses of the men Who have transgressed against Me. For their worm does not die, and their fire is not quenched. They shall be an abhorrence to all flesh*" (Isa. 66:24).

🔥 **The lost will be judged at the Great White Throne** – *"And Then I saw a great white throne and Him who sat on it, from whose face the earth and the heaven fled away. And there was found no place for them. And I saw the dead, small and great, standing before God, and books were opened. And another book was opened, which is the Book of Life. And the dead were judged according to their works, by the things which were written in the books. The sea gave up the dead who were in it, and Death and Hades delivered up the dead who were in them. And they were judged, each one according to his works. Then Death and Hades were cast into the lake of fire. This is the second death. And anyone not found written in the Book of Life was cast into the lake of fire"* (Rev. 20:11-15).

🔥 **People can be saved from the fire** – *"And on some have compassion, making a distinction; 23 but others save with fear, pulling them out of the fire, hating even the garment defiled by the flesh"* (Jude 1:22-23).

🔥 **The fire and punishment are forever** – *"If your hand causes you to sin, cut it off. It is better for you to enter into life maimed, rather than having two hands, to go to hell, into the fire that shall never be quenched--where 'Their worm does not die, and the fire is not quenched'"* (Mark 9:43-44).

51

- **Both the body and soul go to hell** – *"And do not fear those who kill the body but cannot kill the soul. But rather fear Him who is able to destroy both soul and body in hell"* (Matt. 10:28).

- **Hell is a place of wailing and gnashing of teeth** – *"The Son of Man will send out His angels, and they will gather out of His kingdom all things that offend, and those who practice lawlessness, and will cast them into the furnace of fire. There will be wailing and gnashing of teeth"* (Matt. 13:41-42).

- **The lost will hear the words, "Depart from me"** – *"Then He will also say to those on the left hand, 'Depart from Me, you cursed, into the everlasting fire prepared for the devil and his angels"* (Matt. 25:41).

- **Anger can lead to hell** – *"But I say to you that whoever is angry with his brother without a cause shall be in danger of the judgment. And whoever says to his brother, 'Raca!' shall be in danger of the council. But whoever says, 'You fool!' shall be in danger of hell fire"* (Matt. 5:22).

- **Being religious isn't enough to save you from hell** – *"Woe to you, scribes and*

Pharisees, hypocrites! For you are like whitewashed tombs which indeed appear beautiful outwardly, but inside are full of dead men's bones and all uncleanness. Even so you also outwardly appear righteous to men, but inside you are full of hypocrisy and lawlessness. Woe to you, scribes and Pharisees, hypocrites! Because you build the tombs of the prophets and adorn the monuments of the righteous, and say, 'If we had lived in the days of our fathers, we would not have been partakers with them in the blood of the prophets.' Therefore, you are witnesses against yourselves that you are sons of those who murdered the prophets. Fill up, then, the measure of your fathers' guilt. Serpents, brood of vipers! How can you escape the condemnation of hell?" (Matt. 23:27-33).

🔥 Judgment and hell are guaranteed to those who are evil – *"But For if God did not spare the angels who sinned, but cast them down to hell and delivered them into chains of darkness, to be reserved for judgment...and did not spare the ancient world, but saved Noah, one of eight people, a preacher of righteousness, bringing in the flood on the world of the ungodly; and turning the cities of Sodom and Gomorrah into ashes, condemned them to destruction, making them an example to those who afterward would live un- godly... then the Lord knows how to deliver the godly out of temptations and to reserve the unjust under punishment for the day of judgment, and*

53

especially those who walk according to the flesh in the lust of uncleanness and despise authority. They are presumptuous, self-willed. They are not afraid to speak evil of dignitaries" (2 Pet. 2:4-6, 9-10).

🔥 **Jesus has the key to death and hell** – *"If I am He who lives, and was dead, and behold, I am alive forevermore. Amen. And I have the keys of Hades and of Death"* (Rev. 1:18).

🔥 **The parable of the rich man and Lazarus** – *"There was a certain rich man who was clothed in purple and fine linen and fared sumptuously every day. But there was a certain beggar named Lazarus, full of sores, who was laid at his gate, desiring to be fed with the crumbs which fell from the rich man's table. Moreover, the dogs came and licked his sores. So it was that the beggar died, and was carried by the angels to Abraham's bosom. The rich man also died and was buried. And being in torments in Hades, he lifted up his eyes and saw Abraham afar off, and Lazarus in his bosom. Then he cried and said, 'Father Abraham, have mercy on me, and send Lazarus that he may dip the tip of his finger in water and cool my tongue; for I am tormented in this flame.' But Abraham said, 'Son, remember that in your lifetime you received your good things, and likewise Lazarus evil things; but now he is comforted* *and you are tormented. And besides all this, between us and you there is a great gulf fixed, so that those who want to pass from here to you cannot, nor can those from there pass to us.' Then he said, 'I beg you therefore, father, that you would send him to my father's house, for I have five brothers, that he may testify to them, lest they also come to this place of torment.' Abraham said to him, 'They have Moses and the prophets; let them hear them.' And he said, 'No, father Abraham; but if one goes to them from the dead, they will repent.' But he said to him, 'If they do not hear Moses and the prophets, neither will they be persuaded though one rise from the dead"* (Luke 16:19-31).

♦ **Those who worship the beast and receive his mark will be tormented in hell forever** – *"Then a third angel followed them, saying with a loud voice, "If anyone worships the beast and his image, and receives his mark on his fore- head or on his hand, he himself shall also drink of the wine of the wrath of God, which is poured out full strength into the cup of His indignation. He shall be tormented with fire and brimstone in the presence of the holy angels and in the presence of the Lamb. And the smoke of their torment ascends forever and ever; and they have no rest day or night, who worship the beast and his image, and whoever receives the mark of his name"* (Rev. 14:9-11).

🔥 **Hell is for the wicked** – *"The wicked shall be turned into hell, and all the nations that forget God"* (Ps. 9:17).

🔥 **Hell is a place of outer darkness** – *"The sons of the kingdom will be cast out into outer darkness. There will be weeping and gnashing of teeth"* (Matt. 8:12).

🔥 **Judgment is given according to their portion** – *"But if that evil servant says in his heart, 'My master is delaying his coming,' and begins to beat his fellow servants, and to eat and drink with the drunkards, the master of that servant will come on a day when he is not looking for him and at an hour that he is not aware of, and will cut him in two and appoint him his portion with the hypocrites. There shall be weeping and gnashing of teeth"* (Matt. 24:48-51).

🔥 **People are cast into hell** – *"If your hand or foot causes you to sin, cut it off and cast it from you. It is better for you to enter into life lame or maimed, rather than having two hands or two feet, to be cast into the everlasting fire. And if* *your eye causes you to sin, pluck it out and cast it from you. It is better for you to enter into life with one eye, rather than having two eyes, to be cast into hell fire"* (Matt. 18:8-9).

♦ **Hell will be a place a weeping** – *"Then the king said to the servants, 'Bind him hand and foot, take him away, and cast him into outer darkness; there will be weeping and gnashing of teeth"* (Matt. 22:13).

♦ **The unprofitable go to hell** – *"For to everyone who has, more will be given, and he will have abundance; but from him who does not have, even what he has will be taken away. 30 And cast the unprofitable servant into the outer darkness. There will be weeping and gnashing of teeth"* (Matt. 25:29-30).

♦ **Those without a relationship with Christ will be thrust out** – *"But He will say, 'I tell you I do not know you, where you are from. Depart from Me, all you workers of iniquity.' 28 There will be weeping and gnashing of teeth, when you see Abraham and Isaac and Jacob and all the prophets in the kingdom of God, and yourselves thrust out"* (Luke 13:27-28).

♦ **Hell is like a pit** – *"You shall be brought down to Sheol, To the lowest depths of the Pit"* (Isa. 14:15).

57

7

Who Goes to Hell?

Amazingly, the Bible mentions hell some 167 times. Other names for hell are: Gehenna, Hades, the pit, the Abyss, or everlasting punishment. Speaking about the *"crafty harlot,"* Proverbs 7:27 says, *"Her house is the way to hell, Descending to the chambers of death."* In Luke 8:31 hell is described as *"The Abyss."* Further on in Luke's gospel, the word, Hades is used. Paul speaks of hell in 2 Thessalonians 1:9, as *"Everlasting punishment."*

58

Jesus spoke of hell more than all other biblical writers. R.C. Sproul said, "Jesus talks about hell more than he talks about heaven, and describes it more vividly. There's no denying that Jesus knew, believed, and warned against the absolute reality of hell." Clearly, Jesus wanted to make sure we understand that hell is real place (See Matt. 13:41–42; 23:33; Mark 9:43–47; Luke 12:5).

In the story about a rich man and a beggar named Lazarus, Jesus illustrates, which I believe was an actual event, the reality of the two eternal destinations. Check out the fascinating story in Luke 16:19–31. In the story, Jesus describes a great chasm (a large span or gap) over which *"none may cross from there to us."* Two people groups are represented, one on each side of the chasm. In the gospel of Matthew, chapter 25, Jesus tells of a time when people will be separated into these two groups, one entering into his presence, the other banished to "eternal destruction, the eventually to eternal fire.

One writer explains it like this, "The doctrine of hell is uncomfortable for most of us. However, our understanding of hell shapes our view of the gospel, God's holiness, and our depravity. If we don't accept the reality of hell, we won't rightly understand the glory of the gospel."

Biblically, Heaven is the dwelling place of God (2 Chron. 30:27). Heaven is where Jesus has gone to *"prepare a place"* for those who love Him (John 14:2). Hell, on the other hand, was created for *"the devil and his angels"* (Matthew 25:41). Here's the really bad news, since every human being is a sinner, every person past the age of accountability has already been condemned to hell (Romans 3:10; 5:12; John 3:18). Therefore, we all deserve hell as the just punishment for our rebellion against God (Romans 6:23).

8

The 8-Lane Highway to Hell

"The road to hell is paved with good intentions."
–Saint Bernard of Clairvaux

The Broad Road is the 8-Lane Highway

As a young minister, pastoring my first church. Roy Bay was one of the senior saints in the congregation. One day he walked into the local Denny's Restaurant as I was having coffee.

I invited him to sit down, and it became a regular thing soon after. We would talk about the Bible, the good old days, and the church. He loved to talk about the end-times, me too. Quickly, we hit it off. I loved hanging out with brother Bay, as I called him. He was one of the early friendships I developed in Humboldt County. He has since passed on to be with the Lord. I miss him and often reflect on his words about the good old days when church life was more straightforward than it is today.

One day he asked me if I had ever heard of the 8-Lane Highway. I hadn't, so he shared with me what the Lord had given him years before. Shortly after that, I preached a sermon series titled the 8-Lane Highway with Roy's blessing. After he passed, several years later, the Lord impressed upon me to write this book. I want to thank brother Roy Bay, who is in heaven, for his inspiration. Here is the verse brother Bay shared with me.

Revelation 21:8

"The cowardly, unbelieving, abominable, murderers, sexually immoral, sorcerers, idolaters, and all liars shall have their part in the lake which burns with fire and brimstone, which is the second death."

This verse speaks of eight sins leading to the lake of fire and the second death. The first death is physical (Matt. 10:28). Those who die without Christ are doomed to face the second death, when the spiritually dead are "Cast into the lake of fire" (Rev. 20:14). The unfortunate who dies on the 8-Lane Highway, never finding the narrow gate, become eternally separated from God (2 Thess. 1:9). They are the unsaved and "Unbelievers" (2 Cor. 6:14). Fortunate is those who find Christ and the narrow road. The Bible says, "Blessed and holy is he who has part in the first resurrection. Over such the second death has no power, but they shall be priests of God and of Christ, and shall reign with Him a thousand years" (Rev. 20:6).

Make no mistake about it; the broad road is the 8-Lane Highway. These lanes, these sins, are lifestyles. All people, in Christ or apart for Him, must be forewarned. Destruction awaits all who live or dabble on this road. The victims of sin, which pulls us away from God, end up traveling on the lanes of this highway.

THE 8-LANE HIGHWAY:

Lane One

The Cowardly – *"Therefore whoever confesses Me before men, him I will also confess before My Father who is in heaven. ³³ But whoever denies Me before men, him I will also deny before My Father who is in heaven"* (Matt. 10:32-33).

Lane Two

The Unbelieving – *"Beware, brethren, lest there be in any of you an evil heart of unbelief in departing from the living God…"* (Heb. 3:12).

Lane Three

The Abominable – *"For the perverse person is an abomination to the Lord, but His secret counsel is with the upright"* (Prov. 3:32).

Lane Four

The Murderers – *"The wicked watches the righteous, And seeks to slay him"* (Ps. 37:32).

Lane Five

The Sexually Immoral – *"Flee sexual immorality. Every sin that a man does is outside the body, but he who commits sexual immorality sins against his own body"* (1 Cor. 6:18).

Lane Six

The Sorcerers – *"And I will come near you for judgment; I will be a swift witness against sorcerers, against adulterers, against perjurers, against those who exploit wage earners and widows and orphans…because they do not fear Me, says the Lord of hosts"* (Mal. 3:5).

Lane Seven

The Idolators – *"For this you know, that no fornicator, unclean person, nor covetous man, who is an idolater, has any inheritance in the kingdom of Christ and God"* (Eph. 5:5).

Lane Eight

The Liars – *"For "He who would love life and see good days, let him refrain his tongue from evil, And his lips from speaking deceit"* (1 Pet. 3:10).

Life? or Destruction?
Only Two Ways to enter:

Matthew 7:13-14

"Enter by the narrow gate; for wide is the gate and broad is the way that leads to destruction, and there are many who go in by it. Because narrow is the gate and difficult is the way which leads to life, and there are few who find it."

9

How to Miss Going to Hell

God will require justice for his blood from those who do not believe in him" –Polycarp, AD 120-165

Hell is no joking matter. Biblically, the fool says, in his heart, *"There is no God"* (Ps. 14:1). Unfortunately, unbelievers can only mock Hell as they deny its existence. If you don't believe in God, why would you believe in the Hell He created. Unfortunately, too many today mock Hell and don't take biblical eternity seriously. One guy said, "I hope they serve beer in hell."

In 1966 John Lennon, of the Beatles, during his interview with an American Magazine, made a tragic and mocking comment about Christianity and Jesus. He said: "Christianity will end; it will disappear. I do not have to argue about that. I am certain. Jesus was ok, but his subjects were too simple; today, we are more famous than Him. Many believers knew this was a foolish thing to say. Not long after Lennon made the infamous claim, saying that the Beatles were more famous than Jesus Christ, he was shot six times.

The famous actress and beauty icon Marilyn Monroe made a colossal blunder. One day she got a visit from the Reverend Billy Graham. He showed up during a presentation of a show. Sent by God with a message for her. He said, "The Spirit of God has sent me to preach to you." She quickly rejected the preacher and God, saying, "I don't need your Jesus." Strangely, a week later, she was found dead in her apartment.

I don't know why John Lennon or Marilyn Monroe made that foolish statement. I don't know if they are in Heaven or Hell. Why? Because I can't possibly know their hearts; only

God does. However, this I do know, denying Him and rejecting him is a grave matter.

Here is my point, many people, including some who believe in Jesus Christ, will tell you without hesitation, "The Bible isn't real!" "Jesus isn't real!" "Hell isn't real!" "Hell isn't for me," They will declare, not understanding anything about it. These people falsely believe and are convinced that what you think means more than what you do. Hell is a real place; billions will go there simply because they believe in God and forget everything else. Hell is for those who "die in their sins" (John 8:24).

Yes, it's good to believe in God. But God is NOT the door, and believing in God alone is not enough to save you. For "*Even the demons believe in God...*" (James 2:19), and they, being evil, certainly are not invited to Heaven. There is only one way to lock behind you, the gate to Hell. You need the key, God's unique key. There is only one, and you MUST acquire it.

Jesus has the key that locks Hell and opens Heaven. Here is the key to Heaven; Jesus Christ is the Door. Yes, they are One, the Father, the Son, and the Holy Spirit. But the door to Heaven and eternal life goes through the Son of God, Jesus.

It is vitally important to listen to what Jesus says about Himself and have enteral life. These are the words of Christ Himself and those who followed Him as they wrote down His words. Believe in these words, and you will be changed.

† **Jesus has the key** – *"I am He who lives, and was dead, and behold, I am alive forevermore. Amen. And I have the keys of Hades and of Death"* (Rev. 1:18).

† **Believe in Jesus** – *"You believe in God, believe also in me"* (John 10:9).

† **Jesus is the door** – *"I am the door. If anyone enters by Me, he will be saved, and will go in and out and find pasture"* (John 14:6).

† **Jesus is the only way** – *"Jesus said to him, "I am the way, the truth, and the life. No one comes to the Father except through Me"* (John 14:1-3).

† **He who has the Son has life** – *"He who has the Son has life; he who does not have the Son of God does not have life. These things I have written to you who believe in the name of the Son of God, that you may know that you have eternal life, and that you may continue to believe in the name of the Son of God"* (1 John 5:12-13).

Tragically, the multitudes are living a godless life and are doomed to live for all eternity in eternal flames. But they don't have to, and neither do you. Only the Devil is eager to see you in Hell and the Lake of Fire. Jesus said, "I have come that you might have life…" (John 10:10). He doesn't want anyone to die in their sins. The biblical writer and disciple of Jesus said, "The Lord is not slack concerning His promise, as some count slackness, but is longsuffering toward us, not willing that any should perish but that all should come to repentance" (2 Pet. 3:9).

† **Jesus' desire** – *"... God our Savior, who desires ALL MEN to be saved and to come to the knowledge of the truth"* (1 Timothy 2:4).

† **Jesus' purpose** – *"For the Son of Man has come to seek and to save that which was lost"* (2 Peter 3:9).

† **Jesus' hope** – *"The Lord is not slack concerning His promise, as some count slackness, but is longsuffering toward us, not willing that any should perish but that all should come to repentance"* (2 Peter 3:9).

† **Jesus' declaration** – *"For there is no distinction between Jew and Greek, for the same Lord over all is rich to all who call upon Him. For WHOEVER calls upon the name of the Lord shall be saved"* (Romans 10:12).

With all that being said, what is the secret to missing Hell? How exactly do you find the key, the door, and Jesus? Don't forget your sin brings death (Rom. 6:23) and an infinite and eternal penalty. Someone must pay the price. After all, this is not rocket science; a child can understand.

Therefore, God became a human being in the person of Jesus Christ (John 1:1, 14). In Jesus Christ, God lived among us, taught us, and healed us—but those things were not His ultimate mission. God became a human being so that He could die for us. Jesus, God in human form, paid the price for your sins and died on the cross. As God, His death was infinite and eternal in value, paying the total cost for sin (1 John 2:2).

God invites you, me, and the world to receive Jesus Christ as Lord and Savior. Accepting His death as the full, just, and final payment for all the sins you have and will ever commit in the future, God adopts you and His own. God promises that anyone who believes in Jesus (John 3:16), trusting Him alone as the Savior (John 14:6), will be saved and miss out on Hell.

God does not want anyone to go to Hell (2 Peter 3:9). That is why God made the ultimate, perfect, and sufficient sacrifice on our behalf. So, it's simple, if you do not want to go to Hell, receive Jesus as your Savior. Simple, right? Tell God that you recognize that you are a sinner and deserve to go to Hell. Declare to God, from your heart, that you are trusting in Jesus Christ to save you.

Did you know that once you commit to trusting Christ to save you, Heaven throws a party just for you? Talking about salvation, Jesus said, "*I say to you that likewise there will be more joy in heaven over one sinner who repents than over ninety-nine just persons who need no repentance.*"

To reiterate the way to miss Hell, you MUST be converted, your sins are forgiven, allowing the blood of Jesus to cleanse you. Below is more scriptural proof of what I say. Maybe you will join the millions that have stopped merely gazing through the hole and open the door wide. I hope you will take the time and open the door of your heart and mind today.

† **Repent and turn from your life of sin** — *"Repent therefore and be converted, that your sins may be blotted out, so that times of refreshing may come from the presence of the Lord"* (Acts 3:19).

† **Confess your sins and pray the sinners prayer of repentance** —*"If we confess our sins, he is faithful and just to forgive us our sins and to cleanse us from all unrighteousness"* (1 John 1:9).

† **The two-step process of believing and confessing** — *"... if you <u>confess</u> with your mouth the Lord Jesus and <u>believe</u> in your heart that God has raised Him from the dead, you will*

be saved. For with the heart one believes to righteousness, and with the mouth confession is made to salvation" (Rom. 10:9)

More Salvation Scriptures

† **Salvation through Jesus** – *"Nor is there salvation in any other, for there is no other name under heaven given among men by which we must be saved"* (Acts 4:12).

† **Jesus the Mediator** – *"For there is one God and one Mediator between God and men, the Man Christ Jesus, who gave Himself a ransom for all ..."* (1 Tim. 2:5).

† **Jesus the Life** – *Jesus said to her, "I am the resurrection and the life, he who believes in Me, though he may die, he shall live. And whoever lives and believes in Me shall never die"* (John 11:25).

† **Jesus the Light** – *Then Jesus spoke to them again, saying, "I am the light of the world. He who follows Me shall not walk in darkness, but have the light of life"* (John 8:12).

† **Jesus the Bread of Life** – *And Jesus said to them, "I am the bread of life. He who comes to Me shall never hunger and he who believes in Me shall never thirst"* (John 6:35).

† **The Living Bread** – *"I am the living bread which came down from heaven. If anyone eats of this bread, he will live forever; and the bread that I shall give is My flesh, which I shall give for the life of the world"* (John 6:51).

† **Everlasting Life** – *"... whoever believes in Him should not perish but have eternal life. For God so loved the world that He gave His only begotten Son, that whoever believes in Him should not perish but have everlasting life"* (John 3:15-16).

† **He Who Believes** – *"He who believes in the Son has everlasting life; and he who does not believe the Son shall not see life, but the wrath of God abides on his"* (John 3:36).

† **Don't Die in Your Sins** – *"Therefore I said to you that you will die in your sins; for if you do not believe that I am He, you will die in your sins"* (John 8:24).

† **Pass from Death to Life** – *"Most assuredly, I say to you, he who hears My word and believes in Him who sent Me has everlasting life, and shall not come into judgment, but has passed from death to life"* (John 5:24).

† **Life is in the Son** – *"... And this is the testimony: that God has given us eternal life and this life is in His Son. He who has the Son has*

life; He who does not have the Son of God does not have life" (1 John 5:11).

† **Savior of the World** – *"And we have seen and testify that the Father has sent the Son as Savior of the world. Whoever confesses that Jesus is the Son of God, God abides in him, and he in God"* (1 John 4:14).

10

Why You Need a Relationship with Jesus

Illustrated

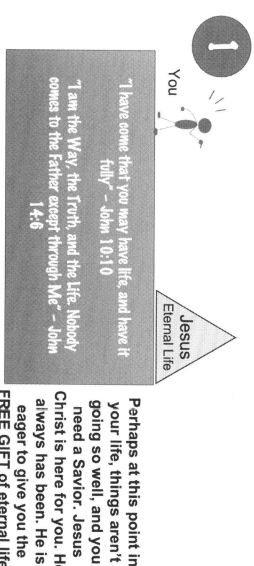

"I have come that you may have life, and have it fully" – John 10:10

"I am the Way, the Truth, and the Life. Nobody comes to the Father except through Me" – John 14:6

You

Jesus
Eternal Life

Perhaps at this point in your life, things aren't going so well, and you need a Savior. Jesus Christ is here for you. He always has been. He is eager to give you the FREE GIFT of eternal life. But there is a serious problem!

...Sin creates a huge separation, a gap. The span is too far; no one can cross it. No one is good enough, can earn their way, or work hard enough to get to the other side. Sin, something we all do, and death, something we all experience keeps us from a relationship with Jesus. But there is hope...

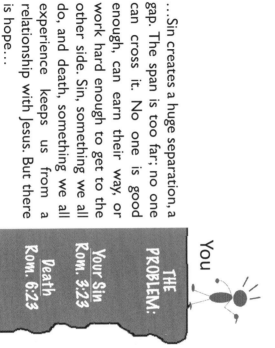

THE GAP

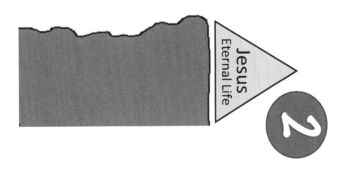

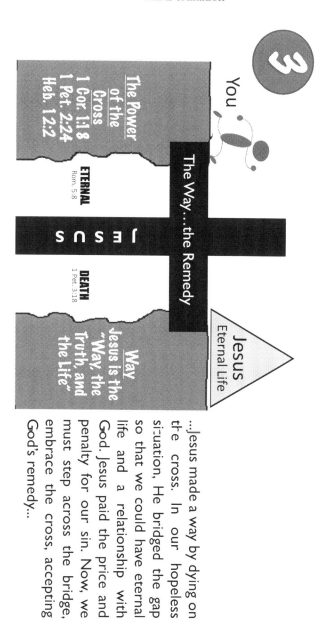

3

You

The Power
of the
Cross
1 Cor. 1:18
1 Pet. 2:24
Heb. 12:2

ETERNAL
Rom. 5:8

The Way...the Remedy

JESUS

DEATH
1 Pet. 3:18

Way
Jesus is the
"Way, the
Truth, and
the Life"

Jesus
Eternal Life

...Jesus made a way by dying on the cross. In our hopeless situation, He bridged the gap so that we could have eternal life and a relationship with God. Jesus paid the price and penalty for our sin. Now, we must step across the bridge, embrace the cross, accepting God's remedy...

81

...by first, believing, in your heart that Jesus Christ rose from the dead. By putting your trust in Him as your Savior. This means a decision of the heart to live for Him completely. Secondly, by declaring your faith in Him through true repentance of your sins. This means to turn away from sin and turn toward God.

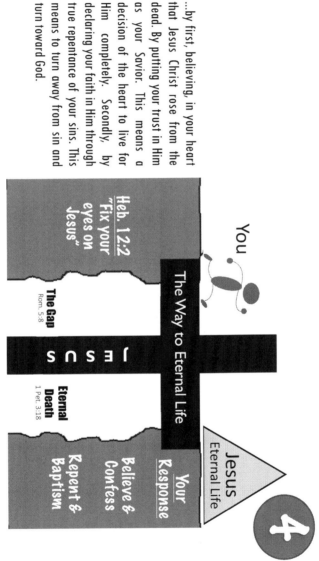

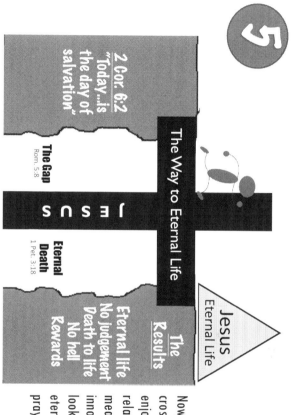

The Way to Eternal Life

2 Cor. 6:2
"Today...is the day of salvation"

The Gap
Rom. 5:8

JESUS

Eternal Death
1 Pet. 3:18

Jesus
Eternal Life

The Results

Eternal life
No Judgement
Death to life
No hell
Rewards

Now, all you have to do is crossed the bridge. Then you can enjoy the benefits of a new relationship with Jesus. This means, eternal life, standing innocent before God, and looking forward to all of eternity in HEAVEN. It's time to pray...

83

What's Next?

…The Sinner's Prayer: Now that you have a clearer understanding, it's time to pray and invite Jesus into your heart and life. Pray this simple prayer to begin a new relationship with Jesus: *"Dear Jesus, I'm sorry for my sin. I thank you for dying to take all of my sins away. I repent and confess my faith in you to save me. I know I cannot save myself. Jesus I ask you to come into my life and be my savior. Help me to live strong in my new relationship with you. Help me to know you more each day. I pray this prayer in the name of Jesus Christ. Amen!"*

Your Final Destination

DID YOU KNOW THAT GOD HAS AN AWESOME PLAN FOR YOU?

(Keep Reading)

God has a Plan for You

"God says, 'At the right time I heard your prayers. On the day of salvation I helped you.' I tell you that the 'right time' is now, and the 'day of salvation' is now" –2 Cor. 6:2 (NCV)

His P.L.A.N.

A SIMPLE WAY TO BECOME A BELIEVER IN JESUS CHRIST

You need a **PLACE** to go – Jesus assured us, *"I go to prepare a place for you"* (John 14:2). The place He is referring to is heaven, where the Father is. Something powerful happens when you believe, by faith, in Jesus Christ. The Bible says it like this, *"Most assuredly, I say to you, he who hears My word and believes in Him who sent Me has everlasting life, and shall not come into judgment, but has passed from death into life"* (John 5:24).

GOD'S PROMISE:
To prepare a wonderful, beautiful place, for you to go someday.

87

You need to be **LOVED** – No one can love you like God does. John 3:16 says, *"For God so loved the world that He gave His only begotten Son, that whoever believes in Him should not perish but have everlasting life."* Nothing can separate you from His love (Rom. 8:38). God's greatest desire is a relationship with you here on earth and in heaven. Jesus said, *"Behold, I stand at the door and knock. If anyone hears My voice and opens the door, I will come in to him and dine with him, and he with Me. To him who overcomes I will grant to sit with Me on My throne, as I also overcame and sat down with My Father on His throne"* (Rev. 3:20-21).

GOD'S PROMISE:
A special relationship with you through Jesus Christ His Son.

You need an **ANTIDOTE** for sin – There is a poison flowing though mankind, called sin. Sin is the poison working through your body to destroy you and your future. The Bible says, *"All have sinned and fall short of God's glory"* (Rom. 3:23). If sin were a job, the wages would be death (Rom. 6:23). Jesus and His love are the antidote for the sin in your life. *"Love will cover a multitude of sins"* (1 Peter 4:7-8).

GOD'S PROMISE:
To forgive all your sins and help you through this life.

You need a Savior **NOW** – The Bible says, *"Today is the day for salvation"* (2 Cor. 6:2). God's plan for you is real and He desires that it starts now, today. You're need for a Savior is real. That is why Jesus came to the earth, *"To seek and to save what was lost"* (Luke 19:10). Being saved begins with a relationship with Jesus and is the greatest thing in the world. By making Jesus your Lord and Savior, He will forgive your past, transform your present, and make your future secure. Yes, God has a tremendous plan for you; a plan effecting your past, present, and especially your future. Long ago God made this declaration to you: *"I know the plans I have for you, plans to prosper you and not to harm you, plans to give you hope and a future"* (Jer. 29:11 NIV).

GOD'S PROMISE:
To be your personal Savior. To give you freedom from the past, help for the present and the most amazing future in heaven.
(you're next step on the next page)

YOU'RE NEXT STEP!

PRAY THIS SIMPLE PRAYER BY FAITH:
Jesus, I ask you into my heart. Thank you for dying on the cross for me. Please, forgive me of all my sins. I ask you to be my Lord and Savior. Thank you for saving me, today. Now, help me to live by faith. Amen."

About the Author

Rev. Danny L. Formhals Sr. has been in full-time ministry for 30+ years. He is a pastor, author, singer, husband, and father. Currently, Danny lives with his wife in Fruitland, Idaho, where he serves as the lead pastor of the Highway Worship Center Church.

Danny is available for ministry

CONTACT INFORMATION
Email:
PastorDLFormhals@gmail.com
For orders: *Amazon.com*
OR
Visit Danny's Website @
DannyFormhals.com

Other Books - Descriptions

Moments of Truth

In Moments of Truth, author Danny Formhals Sr. shares the story of inner struggle and his journey to love, forgiveness, and acceptance. Formhals presents stories and biblical principles in Moments of Truth that guide you to the knowledge that God will help you understand the past and deal with the future in a whole new way. Like oxygen, water, and food are vital to the human body, love, forgiveness, and acceptance are to the spirit. Moments of Truth will help you make a real, lasting positive change in your life. Available as an AUDIO BOOK

The 8-Lane Highway

In The 8-Lane Highway, author Danny Formhals Sr. will challenge your faith. This book focuses on three kinds of Christians today: The fallen away ones, the lukewarm church, and the true believer. Each page is a warning to all the believers in Jesus Christ to WAKE UP and get ready because judgment is coming. You'll discover the broad road in a new light. This biblical road is the 8-Lanes and leads to the lake of fire and God's ultimate judgment.

God's Plan for Your Finances

In God's Plan for Your Finances, author Danny Formhals Sr. addresses the Biblical view on giving and tithing. Sadly, too many have rejected, ignored, or haven't yet discovered the power of God's divine principle. Jesus' words, "It is more blessed to give than to receive" will be seen in a new light. From Genesis to Revelation this book will prove God's unique plan for His followers concerning their financial future. God is a giver, what about you?

The Holy Spirit and Fire

In the Holy Spirit and Fire, author Danny Formhals Sr. helps to enlighten the reader regarding the unique and highly misunderstood spiritual gift of tongues. The Father made a PROMISE to His people. As 120 gathered together on the day of Pentecost, they would come to realize the PURPOSE of the promise. They would receive the power of God to become faithful witnesses. When the Holy Spirit fell on each of them, like tongues of fire, the PLAN of God was unleashed. This book will help the reader understand the Biblical plan to baptize all believers with The Holy Spirit and fire.

Thirsty for Water

Jesus is asking, "Is anyone thirsty?" There is one kind of water that satisfies completely. Author Danny Formhals Sr. draws the believer to a deeper thirst for Jesus, who is the Word, which is the water that brings life. Those who are thirsty will: Walk on the water, ask for water, touch the water, eat the water, and run to the water. Jesus said, "To all who are thirsty I will give freely from the springs of the water of life." Are you, Thirsty for Water?

The Believers Boot Camp

All Christians are fighting in a war. Our commanding officer, the one in charge is the Lord. As soldiers in the Lord's army, we must learn to follow His every command. As an effective soldier for Christ, each participant must be trained up in righteousness. Author Danny Formhals Sr. shares seven basics of the Christian faith. The Believers Boot Camp is necessary to strengthen the local church and empower each heart.

On Fire Stories and Illustrations

Everyone loves a good story. Everyone needs a good story. A story is like a fire it changes everything! In On Fire Stories and Illustrations, author Danny Formhals Sr. jam packs 238 compelling, touching, funny, and informative stories and illustrations into one place. As communicators, speakers, and church leaders, if you're going to have a story to tell, have a big one. This Bible-based resource is useful for sermon preparation, Bible studies, and great talks. Like Jesus, the greatest storyteller of all time, TELL A STORY AND CHANGE A LIFE!

Grieving like a King

In 1 Thessalonians 4:13, the Apostle Paul shares a secret with the grieving church. He tells them, "Brothers and sister, we want you to know what will happen to the believers who have died so you will not grieve like people who have no hope" Sadly, over 8 million individuals in the United States suffer through the death of a loved one. Every year, there are over 800,000 new widows and widowers in the USA. In Grieving like a King, author Danny Formhals Sr. explains how the Lord showed him how to properly grieve the loss of his late wife of 24 years. The reader will discover (1) two systems of grief: The Worlds and the Words. (2) Grieving from King David's perspective. (3) Biblically: who grieved, how long did they grieve, and in what ways did they grieve. (4) The author's do's and don'ts list for the grieving believers. This book is not only for those who are currently mourning but for those needing to prepare others to grieve.

Angels of God

A recent poll published in Time Magazine revealed that 69% of Americans believe in angels, and 46% feel they have a personal guardian angel. The word angel comes from the Greek word *aggelos*; which means "messenger." In Angels of God, author Danny Formhals Sr. shares six compelling thoughts about angels. 18 traditional accounts of angels in Scripture, the only four angelic names mentioned in the Bible, the nine levels of angelic hierocracy, if guardian angels exist, evil and fallen angels in the Bible, and several compelling stories about those who have entertained angels.

Old, Wrinkled, and Closer to Heaven

In Old, Wrinkled, and Closer to Heaven author, Danny Formhals Sr. compiles stories, quotes, humor, and biblical passages celebrating the wonderful seniors in our churches and society. The reader will laugh and be inspired by getting old. The stories, humor, and quotes will have the reader laughing with joy, and the Bible verses will prove how valuable our seniors are to individuals, families, and society.

In the Hand of God

In 2010 author Danny Formhals Sr. had a vision about the hand of God. He saw a vision of what God's hands looked like. He received this vision as his wife Michele was in the hospital suffering from pneumonia and the lingering effects of her seasons of sickness. In the Hand of God will bring the reader strength and encouragement through each trial that arises. Understanding what God does in the process of suffering, trials, challenging situations, and in life, in general, is a powerful ally. Everyone suffers. Job in the Bible knew this best. It was Job who said, "I will teach you about the hand of God." This book is a tool to teach God's people about the loving Father and His hand (s). As you follow the journey of Michele Formhals, you will discover her courage, faith, and trust, as she learned to live in the hand of God. This book is part 1 of the 3-part HAND OF GOD SERIES.

Amazing Young People

In his book, Amazing Young People Author Danny Formhals Sr. writes a 31-day devotional book for youth people and young Christians. It's a book that was written about teenagers and for teenagers. Teenagers are one of the most misunderstood people groups in America and the world. Each daily (devotional) consists of seven parts. (1) A keyword topic to explore with definition (2) a personal story by the author (3) A Bible story about a young person in Scripture to read (4) a section where the author ties everything together, with encouraging words (5) A set of 4 questions to answer and space provided to write answers (6) a quote of the day and (7) Several additional Bible verses to look up and study relating to the topic. Reading this book students, young adults, and young believers will be challenged to live a better life for Christ. Who better to teach our young people, than the Lord and other young found in the pages of the Bible.

Living in the Hand of God

There are over 120 Bible verses that speak of God's hand. None say, "Hands of God." In Living in the Hand of God, you will discover the sixteen verses that use the phrase, "HAND OF GOD." Inside you'll discover how to survive and even thrive in the midst of your trials, pain, and suffering. You'll gain valuable information as you study the life of God's Extraordinary Believers (23 in all), found in the book of Hebrews. You'll also learn about the amazing modern-day vision the author received in 2010 when he saw what God's hands looked like. You'll understand how the hands of God operated to help you be successful every day. As you read, you'll see the hands of God, and you'll discover that suffering can be a powerful ally. The Bible declares, *"But now, O LORD, You are our Father, We are the clay, and You our potter; And all of us are the work of Your hand"* (Isaiah 64:8). Living in the Hand of God is part-2 of the 3-part HAND OF GOD SERIES.

Trusting in the Hand of God

In Trusting in the Hand of God, author D.L. Formhals Sr. elaborates on a vision he had when God showed him a picture of His hands. He began to see God's involvement in our daily lives differently. In this book, you'll discover that the Heavenly Father uses anything and everything to lead us towards His Son Jesus and eternal life. You'll be shocked to learn that evil, sickness, and death are God's tools, as well as trials, pain, and suffering. God's methods, we read about in the Bible, He still uses today. So, get ready to be shaken and challenged to your core regarding what you know about God's Word. This book is a profound journey into the Word of God, and the whole truth about God's direct hand in our lives. Trusting in the Hand of God is part 3 of the 3-part HAND OF GOD SERIES.

The Eleven 11 Project

After a God-given dream, author Danny Formhals Sr. was instructed by the Lord to write The Eleven 11 Project. Inside this book are 11 unique challenges, from the Lord. Each of the 11 challenges will inspire you to walk like Jesus walked, to strive for perfection, and be a stronger wiser believer. The Father's desire is that we become like His Son Jesus Christ. It's time for those who love Jesus to be more like Jesus. It's time to walk as He walked (1 John 2:6). In Matthew 5:48 (AMP) "You, therefore, must be perfect [growing into complete maturity of godliness in mind and character, having reached the proper height of virtue and integrity], as your heavenly Father is perfect."

L.O.S.T. People Matter

The battle for the souls of mankind still rages today. Jesus left us very clear instructions, but, are we doing what He said? Are pastors and the local church fulfilling the Great Commission? In the battle, one of the targets is the Local Church, the heart of souls of God's operation and strategy. Statistics declare that more and more people are falling into the mindset that the local church has become irrelevant today. This attitude must change. L.O.S.T. People Matter is an easy-to-use strategy for the local church. Four important keys will help Leadership, Outreach, Servanthood, and Togetherness. These are essential to winning the lost and helping the local church be what God intends.

Why Jesus Wept

EVERYONE WAS WEEPING. Standing at the tomb of His dear friend, "Jesus wept" (John 11:35). Lazarus had to die so the "Glory of God" (John 11:4) would be revealed through Jesus Christ.

We all weep, cry and suffer from broken hearts. Often time, our broken hearts and mourning are a part of God's plan to reveal Jesus through your brokenness. This book answers the question, Why Jesus wept. And, what breaks the heart of God.

What about Dinosaurs

Even wonder how dinosaurs fit into the Creation story in the Bible. Evolutionists and many Christians do not believe they do. But, what about the person that believes in a literal six-day creation? Is there room for dinosaurs and millions of years in the Bible? This book will show you what possibly happened to the dinosaurs. It's a great informative read for everyone. You will discover the different views between what evolutionists say, what history shows, and how the Bible fits dinosaurs into history. The reader will discover when God's created them, how they died off, how they walked with man, and how history has depicted them.

Walking in a New Way of Life

Walking in a daily relationship with Jesus Christ is imperative for today's born-again believer. Too many live according to how they feel (emotionally led). And far too many follow their own fleshly (worldly) desires. Doing this creates believers who are always under attack by the kingdom of darkness. We must walk as Jesus walked, imitating His life. In this book, author, and pastor Danny L. Formhals Sr. shares ten essential ways to walk with Jesus every day. The Bible says, *"Whoever claims to live in him must walk as Jesus did"* (1 John 2:6 NIV). This book provides ten practical and Biblical ways to help you walk like Jesus.

OMEGA DAYS – A World on Edge

The world is on edge over the greatest terror attack in the history of the planet. Who is behind the attacks, terrorists, or a deeper, sinister foe? Jeremiah Praxis and his guardian angel Darius race to survive the global threat, and to understand their part with CORE, a secret global organization. Was CORE's recruitment of Jeremiah an accident or a part of a greater plan? As the world races towards the Return of Christ, time is running out for Jeremiah and his family to unlock God's plan for their lives. They must battle the power of darkness which has unleashed a devious plot to destroy the United States of America and to get the world ready for the new world order (This is books 1 and 2 in the ONE WORLD SERIES).

OMEGA DAYS – The Beginning of the End

In two short months, the world got ravished by the effects of a mega-tsunami. Nothing will ever be the same again. CORE and the United Nations are bent on the demise of the USA, and plot to end her sovereignty. A secret organization, using the terrorist group, the IWC unleashes waves two and three on the US. Will she survive the onslaught? What is the fate of the USA? Will Jeremiah Praxis and his team of angels figure out the evil scheme behind it all? Will Jeremiah choose to follow God, or will he continue to support Alexander Sirkoff, a man with a hidden agenda to take over the world? What will happen when to the world when the Rapture of the Church strikes? But this is only the beginning of the end because God the Father has unfinished business with the world (This book is parts 3-5 in the ONE WORLD SERIES."

Strange Phenomenon's

Newly appointed FBI Special Agent Luke Doggit accepts the task of establishing a new unit, called Strange Phenomenon's (SP1). Luke and his team are called upon to solve the strange and mysterious cases; that no serious FBI agent wants. It all begins when a strange man shows up in a small Northern California town warning the residents about an impending flood, then seems to disappear. As the small task force tries to unravel the case, more surprises await them. Is it the same man appearing and disappearing all over the country, and why is there a biblical pattern emerging? As the Director of the FBI grows concerned, what will Luke and his team discover about the mysterious man, named Enoch? Who is this man and what are his mysterious plans?

ONE WORLD #1 – Wave of Terror

While America and the world has been rocked. With a Mega-Tsunami and quickly advances into chaos, Jeremiah Praxis, a loving husband and father is struggling with his faith and his involvement with CORE. Is he a pawn in their evil plan to rule the world, or does God have a greater plan for his future? Along with his family, friends, and his team of unseen guardian angels, they race to uncover the truth behind the terrorist attacks and his longtime involvement with CORE. Before it's too late, Jeremiah must decide to stay with CORE or get out.

ONE WORLD #2 – Wave of Destruction

The La Palma Island Mega-tsunami has begun to alter the globe. The coastal regions of many nations have been greatly damaged or destroyed. Everyone waits in horror as the first wave approaches the United States. The prediction is total destruction for the East Coast of the country. The IWC, terrorist have claimed responsibility, and plan two more major attacks on the country. Jeremiah Praxis strives to understand the true motive of CORE, the organization he serves. What part does Jeremiah and his guardian angel play in the global story unfolding before them? As the spirit of fear grips the minds, the hearts, and lives of all Americans, Jeremiah fights to discover the darkness verses the light; is he an agent for evil or for good? Only the coming wave of destruction can answer his questions. Nothing can change what is coming, but how will the coming wave of destruction, change everything?

ONE WORLD #3 – Eagle Down

A Mega-Tsunami rocked America and many countries. Two states and most of the East Coast are gone. The world's people are riddled with fear as a force more powerful than any army has taken control. The people of the United States and the world are shaken to their core. They wonder why the IWC terror group is claiming responsibility for the ten massive waves of destruction. Is the IWC, the Islamic World Caliphate, the masterminds behind it all? How are they connected to the secret group known as CORE, and why are they plotting to destroy America and bring the great eagle down? In all the chaos, Jeremiah Praxis, a loving husband and father, struggles with his faith and involvement with the secret global organization. Jeremiah and his team of unseen guardian angels race to uncover the truth behind the plot to bring America to her knees. CORE wants a one-world government. Can they be stopped? God's Kingdom and the Kingdom of Satan collide in this 3rd book in the ONE WORLD series on the end-times.

Be Ready!

1 Thessalonians 5:1-4 (NKJV)

"But concerning the times and the seasons, brethren, you have no need that I should write to you. ² For you yourselves know perfectly that the day of the Lord so comes as a thief in the  *night. ³ For when they say, "Peace and safety!" then sudden destruction comes upon them, as labor pains upon a pregnant woman. And they shall not escape. ⁴ But you, brethren, are not in darkness, so that this Day should overtake you as a thief. ⁵ You are all sons of light and sons of the day. We are not of the night nor of darkness. ⁶ Therefore let us not sleep, as others do, but let us watch and be sober."*

Jesus is coming back soon!

Made in the USA
Columbia, SC
05 October 2022

68771645R00059